The
Quotable
TRACTOR

MBI

First published in 2005 by MBI, an imprint of MBI Publishing Company, Galtier Plaza, Suite 200, 380 Jackson Street, St. Paul, MN 55101-3885 USA

MBI titles are also available at discounts in bulk quantity for industrial or sales-promotional use. For details write to Special Sales Manager at MBI Publishing Company, Galtier Plaza, Suite 200, 380 Jackson Street, St. Paul, MN 55101-3885 USA.

All photographs by Randy Leffingwell.

ISBN-13: 978-0-7603-2210-9
ISBN-10: 0-7603-2210-4

Editor: Amy Glaser
Designer: Mandy Iverson

Printed in China

I lived in solitude in the *country*

and noticed how the monotony

of a quiet life *stimulates the creative mind.*

⟡

Albert Einstein

Working on a *car* is a job;

working on an *old tractor*

is recreation.

⊶⊷

Roger Welsch

The *harder you work,* the luckier you get.

❖

Gary Player

Any jackass

can *kick down* a barn,

but it takes a good carpenter

to *build* one.

✛

Sam Rayburn

Treat the earth well.

It was *not* given to you by your parents.

It is lent to you by your children.

—‡—

Kenyan proverb

Burn down your cities

and leave our farms,

and your cities

will spring up again

as if by magic;

but destroy our farms

and the *grass will grow*

in the streets of every city

in the country.

—⁜—

William Jennings Bryan

Adopt the pace of nature:

her *secret is patience.*

⟷

Ralph Waldo Emerson

Make your own sunshine—

it may not tan the skin,

but *it will warm the heart.*

—†—

Anonymous

When you can't have anything else,

you *can have* virtue.

⊷⊦⊶

Don Marquis

The reward of a thing well done *is to have done it.*

⸬

Ralph Waldo Emerson

One touch of nature

makes the *whole world* kin.

William Shakespeare

Nothing is really work

unless you would rather be doing something else.

✣

James M. Barrie

Some men are *always going to make hay*

while the sun shines—

tomorrow.

—†—

Anonymous

Knowing trees,

I *understand* the meaning

of *patience.*

Knowing grass,

I can *appreciate*

persistence.

—

Hal Borland

Can *anybody* remember

when the times were not hard **and** money not scarce?

＊ー￤ー＊

Ralph Waldo Emerson

The farther *backward* you can look,

the farther *forward* you are likely to see.

⊷⊢⊶

Winston Churchill

Our necessities are *few,*

but our wants are *endless.*

⁜

Bernard Shaw

A *job worth doing*

is worth *doing well.*

—

Anonymous

It isn't the hours you put in your work that count,

it's the *work you put in the hours.*

—†—

Anonymous

Our ideals, laws, and customs

should be based on the proposition

that *each generation* in turn

becomes the *custodian*

rather than the absolute owner

of our *resources*—

and *each generation*

has the obligation

to *pass this inheritance on to the future.*

—⁍—

Alden Whitman

The secret of success:

never **let down** and never **let up.**

✦

Anonymous

The earth *is given*

as a common stock

for man to *labor*

and *live* on.

⁘

Thomas Jefferson

Inspiration is everywhere.

If you're ready to appreciate it,

an ant can be one of the

wonders of the universe.

Anonymous

We abuse land

because we regard it

as a commodity

belonging to us.

When we see the land

as a community

to which we belong,

we may begin to use it

with love and respect.

✦

Aldo Leopold

A day spent in the shop

working on an old tractor

doesn't count toward getting older.

God considers it a freebie.

⊷

Roger Welsch

Remote though

your farm may be,

it's something

to be the lord

of one green lizard—

and *free*.

—┼—

Juvenal

Success is getting what you want;

happiness is *wanting what you get.*

﹢

Anonymous

One must stand on his head

to get the best effect

in a fine *sunset,*

to bring out all its beauty.

—⊹—

Mark Twain

Men and Nature must work hand in hand.

The throwing out of balance

of the resources of Nature

throws out of balance

also the lives of men.

—✦—

Franklin D. Roosevelt

I suppose the pleasure

of country life lies really

in the eternally renewed

evidences of

the *determination to live.*

＋

Vita Sackville-West

Into every empty corner,

into all forgotten things and *nooks,*

Nature struggles to pour life,

pouring life into the dead,

life into life itself.

✢

Henry Beston

There is no meaning to life

except the meaning man gives his life

by the unfolding of his powers,

by living productively.

—⚬—

Erich Fromm

Nothing *can bring you peace*

but yourself.

Ralph Waldo Emerson

Civilization

is a limitless multiplication of *unnecessary necessities*.

—‡—

Mark Twain

Work hard.

There is no short cut.

—※—

Alfred P. Sloan Jr

We always admire the *other fellow* more

after we have *tried* to do his job.

✦⊹✦

William C. Feather

Work **sometimes** comes from inspiration,

but more often *inspiration comes from work.*

—✦—

Anonymous

It all depends on *how we look at things,*

and not on how they are in themselves.

∗–†–∗

Carl G. Jung

Nature is *the greatest show on earth.*

⋆—I—⋆

Anonymous

In the event that your mate asks,

"Who do you love more, me or your blasted tractors?"

Whatever you do, don't ask for time to think it over.

—†—

Roger Welsch

One machine can do the work of 50 ordinary men,

but no machine can do the work

of one *extraordinary man.*

—†—

Elbert Hubbard

Let us never forget

that the cultivation

of the earth

is the most important

labor of man.

✢

Daniel Webster

There was **a farmer** who planted some corn.

He said to his neighbor,

"I hope I break even this year.

I really need the money."

＋

John F. Kennedy

If God gave me the choice

of the whole planet

or *my little farm,*

I should certainly

take my farm.

Ralph Waldo Emerson

If we had no winter,

the spring

would not be so pleasant;

if we had not sometimes

taste of adversity,

prosperity

would not be so welcome.

—

Anne Bradstreet

ABOUT THE PHOTOGRAPHER

Randy Leffingwell has more than 30 books in print and is known for his fantastic photography. Leffingwell discovered photography as an architectual engineer student at Kansas Universtiy and hasn't looked back. He lives in Santa Barbara, California, with his wife, Carolyn.